D1389219

recorder

FREDERICK WARNE
Penguin Books Ltd, Harmondsworth,
Middlesex, England
New York, Canada, Australia, New Zealand
First published 1988 by William Heinemann Ltd
Published 1998 by Frederick Warne
10 9 8 7 6 5 4 3 2
Copyright © Eric Hill, 1988
Eric Hill has asserted his moral rights under the
Copyright, Designs and Patents Act of 1988
All rights reserved
ISBN 0 7232 9042 3
Planned and produced by Ventura Publishing Ltd,
27 Wrights Lane, London W8 5TZ
Printed and bound in Singapore by
Tien Wah Press (Pte) Ltd

snail

Spot's Big Book of Words

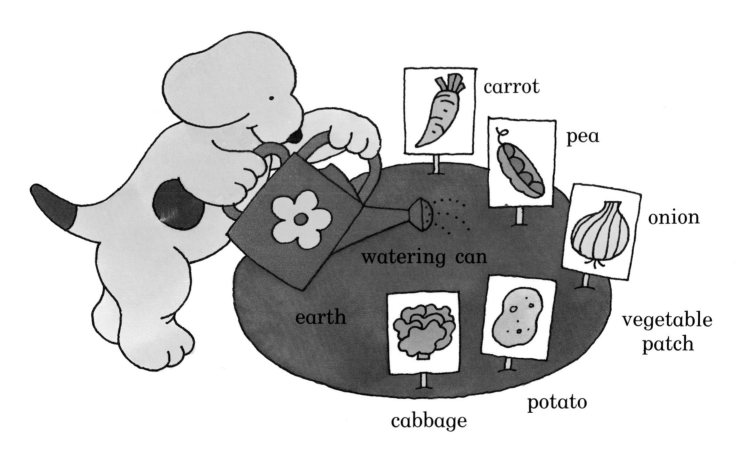

carrot

pea

onion

watering can

earth

vegetable patch

potato

cabbage

Eric Hill

freezer

***

magnets

jug

orange
juice

coffee pot

refrigerator

coffee

spoon

toast

toaster

It's breakfast time
and Spot gets the orange
juice from the refrigerator.
Sally is making cheese
sandwiches for Sam.

cereal

milk jug

bowl

mug

kettle

chimney

roof

farmhouse

sheep

fields

orchard

goose

fence

truck

Spot is helping his dad
on the farm. Tom and Helen
came along to help, but playing
with the wheelbarrow
is more fun.

horn

wheelbarrow

pond

duck

rope

ducklings

stake

frog

hoof

weather vane

dove

horseshoe

barn

wheel

mouse

hay

horse

trailer

stable

tractor

cow

cat

chicken

tail

cockerel

milk bucket

milk churn

pig

clock

blackboard

chalk

teacher

book

bookcase

Spot is at school.
Tom is colouring a picture
with crayons and Spot
and Helen are painting
pictures on their easels.
Soon they will all go
outside to play.

building bricks

ruler

glue

scissors

pencil

rubber

desk

workbook

satchel

crayons

bell

map

swing

slide

lunch box   thermos   tap

see-saw

sink

playground

door

easel   paper

brush

drip

apron

water jar

red   green   paint box   drawing pin   blue   yellow

keyboard

Miss Bear's class is having a music lesson.
Spot thinks it's all great fun – what a noise they're making!

piano

note

guitar

bow

violin

sheet music

harmonica

music stand

triangle

tambourine

recorder

Next door, Helen and Betsy are having a dance lesson. The teacher is going to play some ballet music on the stereo.

record

stereo

stereo speaker

record cover

Swan Lake

stage

steps

star

wand

spotlight

wings

tutu

fairy costume

barre

ballet shoes

cassette player

tape

Tom is painting the shed while Spot waters the vegetable seeds he has planted. Helen has picked some flowers to take home to her mother.

wall

hedge

gate

path

bush

apple tree

worm

leaf

buttercup

apple

butterfly

lawn

flowers

birdbath

basket

flower bed

seagull

rod

Spot is at the beach
and can't wait to get
to the sea! Helen, Steve
and Tom are at the beach, too.
What is Helen looking at
through her telescope?

aeroplane

float

line

hook

seaweed

pier

fish

hat

yacht

waves

surf

telescope

rubber
ring

bucket

steps

anchor

pebbles

suntan lotion

beach bag

plant

front door

feather duster

chair

dust

broom

grandfather clock

staircase

magazine

sofa

cushion

newspaper

It's house-cleaning time and Spot and his friends are helping Sally. Turn off the television, Steve!

mirror

tulips

light switch

curtain

television

vase

telephone

remote control

drawer

footstool

lampshade

chest

table lamp

rug

vacuum cleaner

coffee table

furniture wax

fruit bowl

It's such a fine day! Everyone is out in the park. Look at Tom on his new bicycle!

tennis ball

sun visor

tennis racket

net

roller skates

cap

skipping rope

hand brake

handlebars

pedal

tyre

bicycle

helmet

elbow pad

knee pad

skateboard

headband

earphone

stopwatch

jogging suit

transistor radio

sole

sock

jogging shoes

heel

trampoline

tricycle

It's Spot's birthday and he has invited his friends to a birthday party. How old do you think Spot is today? Count the candles on the cake!

wardrobe

hanger

cupboard

belts

rail

jacket

skirt

blouse

T-shirt

shoes

party dress

jeans

mirror

handbag

drawer

beads

flip-flop

dress

Helen's mother has bought a new dress and sweater for Helen. Do you like pink? Helen does!

box

sweater

cowboy boot

cap

jacket

tie

overalls

shorts

duffel bag

trousers

moccasins

socks

rugby shirt

boots

shirt

rain hat

suitcase

trainers

umbrella

swimming trunks

Spot is helping Steve
pack for a holiday.
Steve can't find a pair
of socks that match.
Look under the drawer,
Steve!

Spot and his friends are enjoying some winter fun. Helen made the snowman and his dog. Spot thinks the dog looks like him!

ski poles

goggles

ski boots

skis

mountains

fur hat

snowball

earmuffs

frozen pond

ice skates

mittens

broom

pipe

snowman

scarf

boots

snowdog

snow

smoke

chimney

fir tree

icicle

log cabin

woolly hat

snowflake

gloves

sledge

robin

footprints

log

Spot is staying overnight
at Tom's house.
Tom wants Spot to share the
bunk bed, but Spot pretends
he is camping out in his
sleeping bag.
Sleep well, Spot!

calendar

MAY
S	M	T	W	T	F	S
1	2	3	4	5	6	7
8	9	10	11	12	13	14
15	16	17	18	19	20	21
22	23	24	25	26	27	28
29	30	31				

pyjamas

pinboard

clock

bedside table

sheet

blanket

slippers

bunk bed

ladder

pillow

shower curtain

cabinet

hook

toothbrush

shower

bath toy

toothpaste

shower cap

sponge

soap

tap

radio

toilet paper

toilet

sink

towel

bath

bath mat

dressing gown

sleeping bag

zip

torch

rucksack

biscuits

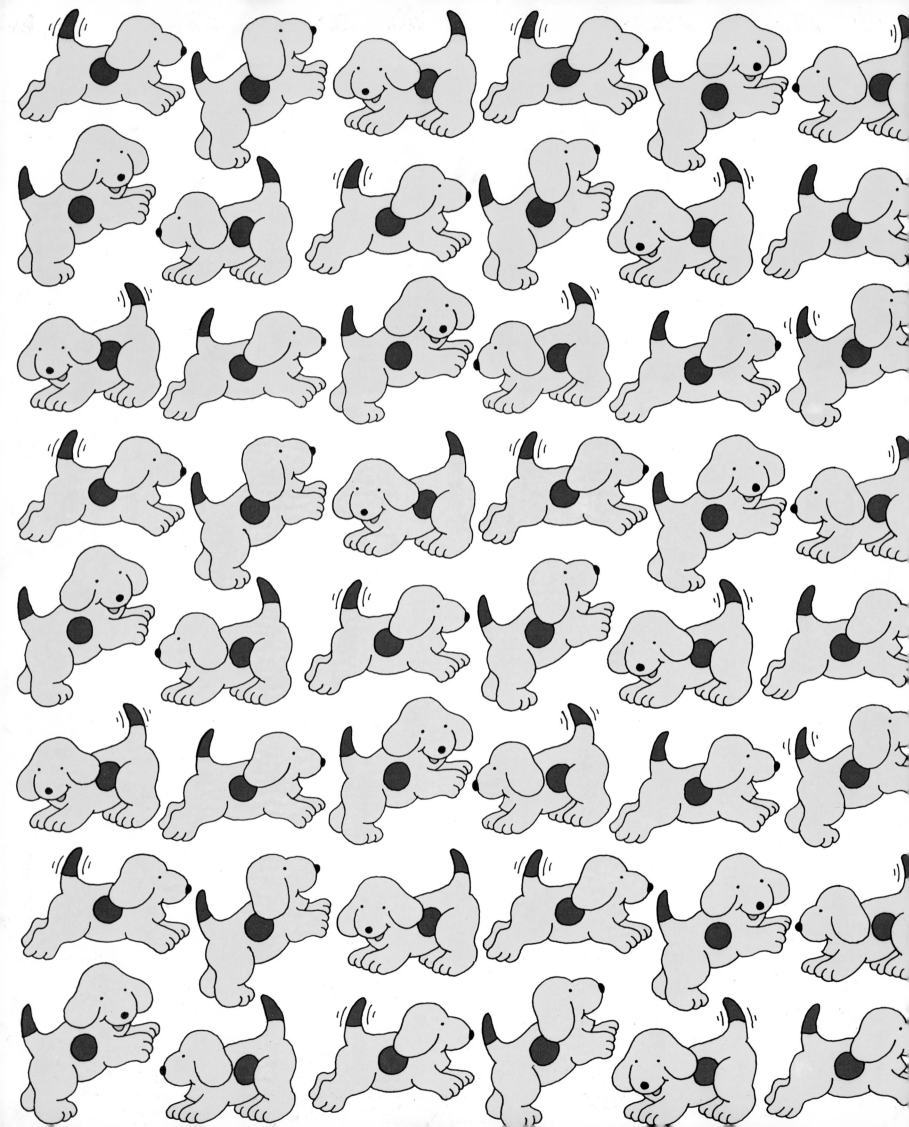